Old Corpus Christi

The Past in Photographs

Edited by
Murphy D. Givens

Presented by the

Corpus Christi Caller Times

Caller.com

c. 1890

Waiting on the front steps of Dr. A.G. Heaney's office on South Bluff.

Murphy Givens Collection

Bayfront, c. 1900
Strollers on the beach.

Table of Contents

Foreword
and
Acknowledgments

The idea for this book was conceived as a way to observe the city's 150th birthday. The intent, whether it succeeds or not, was to tell the story of Corpus Christi's history through photos of the times. There was no question of where to begin. As Alice in Wonderland knew, you begin at the beginning, which in this case was with the earliest photos and drawings available. The question was where to end it. It was finally decided to end it with the building of Harbor Bridge in 1959, an uplifting event which, in many ways, symbolizes the beginning of modern-day Corpus Christi.

This city has more than its share of history. It was a frontier outpost when it became the staging ground for the U.S.-Mexico War. It was a battleground during the Civil War. The cattle industry was born in Corpus Christi's backyard. The people of this city saw the coming of the railroads change the land, they saw the early exploration for oil and gas during the Depression, and they saw the building of the Naval Air Station, which played a major role in World War II. So there is a lot to tell.

Telling this story would have been harder without the work of many photographers, but we must single out three. Louis De Planque (pronounced "plunk") came here in the late 1860s and took thousands of photos of the city and its people for more than three decades. Only a few dozen have survived. William Frederick "Doc" McGregor, a chiropractor, was on his way to California with a Packard full of kids when he stopped for a visit; he never left. "Doc" and his studio employees took up to a million photographs of Corpus Christi, now part of the McGregor Collection at the Corpus Christi Museum of Science and History. Russell Lee was one of the great Depression-era photographers who traveled the country doing documentary photography for the Farm Securities Administration. Lee was in Corpus Christi in the late 1930s and early '40s.

It would have also been even harder to assemble this book without the gracious and unstinting help of Herb Canales and Laura Garcia of Corpus Christi's Central Library, Patricia Murphy at the Corpus Christi Museum of Science and History, and Tom Kreneck and Jan Weaver at Texas A&M University-Corpus Christi. One final note: Some photographs in this volume were chosen for what they reveal about Corpus Christi's history, while others were chosen because they have that little something, that little spark, that makes them, and the past, come alive.

— *Murphy Givens*

CORPUS CHRISTI.

Corpus Christi, 1845

Sketch of Corpus Christi by an unknown artist at the time of Zachary Taylor's encampment, from August 1845 to March 1846. The army's tents were located north of the town.

Caller-Times Archives

Shoreline looking south, 1845
"Camp Marcy," as Zachary Taylor called the encampment in Corpus Christi in preparation for the coming war with Mexico, was captured in a lithograph by Daniel P. Whiting, an officer in Taylor's command.

Louis de Planque/Corpus Christi Central Library

City named for the Bay

Who gave Corpus Christi — "The Body of Christ" — its name? Local tradition has it that Corpus Christi Bay got its name from Spanish explorer Alonzo Alvarez de Pineda who, legend says, sailed into the bay on the feast day of Corpus Christi, 1519. There's little evidence to support that claim. Other Spanish explorers in 1749 — part of the Jose Escandon expedition — called the bay San Miguel Archangel, or Saint Michael the Arch Angel. At some point after that, the bay became known as Corpus Christi Bay.

The earliest name for the settlement on the bluff, overlooking the bay, was Kinney's Rancho, after founder Henry Kinney. In 1841, two years after he built his trading post, Kinney began calling his settlement Corpus Christi. On Sept. 18, 1841, he wrote Mirabeau Lamar, president of the Republic of Texas, and signed the letter, "Kinney's Rancho, Corpus Christi, Texas." It has been called that ever since.

Water Street at Peoples, date unknown

This is one of the earliest photos of Corpus Christi. The building, with its stepped false front, is identified on the back of the photo only as a landmark structure built on the waterfront in 1848. From other sources (including R. Hollub's sketch of the waterfront in 1874), it's believed that this was the Edward Ohler building. The Ohler family lived upstairs and operated a store below.

Corpus Christi Central Library

c. 1860

Henry Lawrence Kinney, a native of Pennsylvania, opened a trading post on the bluff overlooking Corpus Christi Bay in 1839. He served in the Congress of the Republic of Texas and then in the Texas Legislature. He led a failed expedition in the 1850s to create his own "Mosquito Kingdom" in Nicaragua. Kinney, the founder of Corpus Christi, was shot to death in 1862 in Matamoros, Mexico.

Caller-Times Archives

Shoreline, 1862

A sketch by Thomas Noakes shows the high point of the Battle of Corpus Christi on Aug. 18, 1862. U.S. ships in the bay fired at a Confederate battery located near where the ship channel is today. Union forces landed and were repulsed by Confederate cavalry (lower left). The federal fleet under Lt. John Kittredge broke off the action, then bombarded the town as the ships departed.

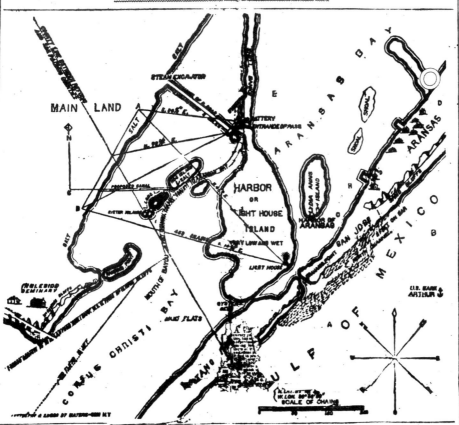

THE NEW YORK HERALD.

WHOLE NO. 9560.   NEW YORK, SUNDAY, NOVEMBER 16, 1862.   PRICE THREE CENTS.

THE CAPTURE OF CORPUS CHRISTI, TEXAS.

Additional Particulars of the Important Operations of the Gunboat Arthur, Captain Kittridge.

EXPLANATION OF CHART.

A report in the *New York Herald Tribune* of Nov. 16, 1862 was not accurate. Corpus Christi was not captured by Union commander Lt. John Kittredge and his flotilla, although the town was bombarded in August, 1862. A different perspective on the battle was reported in Corpus Christi's *Ranchero*, which said the federal ships bombarded the town "and this morning took tail and left Corpus Christi ... being completely foiled and whipped."

Corpus Christi Central Library

c. 1870

Norwick Gussett, a sergeant in the Mexican War, returned to Corpus Christi to begin a freight line. He became a wealthy merchant, banker and rancher. He owned one of the city's largest wool warehouses and a fleet of schooners, which carried wool and hides to New York and brought back merchandise for his store.

Corpus Christi Central Library

c. 1862

Mat Nolan came to Corpus Christi in 1845 with Zachary Taylor's army. He and his brother were Irish orphans who enlisted as bugle boys. After the war, the two became Texas Rangers, and in 1858 Mat was elected sheriff of Nueces County. Tom, as a deputy sheriff, was shot to death while trying to make an arrest in 1860. Mat rose to the rank of colonel in the Confederate Army. In 1864, two Union supporters shot Mat Nolan to death on Mesquite Street, two blocks from where his brother was killed four years before.

c. 1865

George Noessel, born in Germany in 1813, came to Texas in the 1830s. He was captured by Comanches but escaped. He moved to Corpus Christi in the early 1850s, where he and his son Felix operated a store.

Corpus Christi Central Library

Corpus Christi Central Library

c. 1862

Felix A. von Blucher, a self-sketch. Blucher was a Confederate major of engineers and captain of artillery who designed defenses on the Texas Gulf Coast. He took part in the Battle of Corpus Christi in August, 1862. One account said Blucher sighted an 18-pound cannon at one of the federal ships and said, "I believe I'll take a pop at it." He fired and the shell hit near the ship, and he said, "I believe I'll take another one." After that shot, the ship moved out of range.

Caller-Times Archives

c. 1870

Charles Grimus Thorkelin Lovenskiold came to Corpus Christi in 1853 and started the Corpus Christi Academy. He was a Confederate colonel during the Civil War and practiced law after the war.

Bayfront, 1874

Rudoph Hollub, who designed Nueces County's second courthouse, sketched the waterfront in 1874. A schooner and a brig were tied up at the Central Wharf. The large two-story building at the foot of the wharf was Cornelius Cahill's old City Hotel and store.

Central Wharf was located between William and Laguna (now Sartain) streets. The other wharf in the center was Staples Wharf, used to unload shipments of lumber, located at Lawrence Street.

Mesquite Street, 1875

Construction of Nueces County's first courthouse (photo above, building on left) began in 1853. It was designed by Felix A. Blucher, cost $4,000 to build, and took three years to complete. The county's second courthouse (above right, and in the photo at left) was built next to the older structure. It faced Mesquite at Belden Street. The second courthouse was completed in 1875, cost $15,000 to build, and was often called the Hollub Courthouse, after designer and builder Rudolph Hollub. It was replaced by the 1914 courthouse.

MAP
of
THE PUBLIC ROADS OF
NUECES COUNTY
adopted classified and designated by the County Commissioner's Court
of Nueces County, at their regular meeting in February 1879 and
surveyed and marked out by Lafayette Caldwell, Surveyor

Lafayette Caldwell

NUECES RIVER

de la GARZA MONTEMAYOR

ROCKPORT

HARBOR ISLAND

CORPUS CHRISTI BAY

W.W. Wright's Pasture

UP RIVER ROAD

CORPUS CHRISTI & SAN DIEGO RAILROAD

CORPUS-CHRISTI

Rabb's Pasture

LAREDO RD.

W.S.Gregory

CAYA DEL OSO

FLOUR BLUFFS

MUSTANG ISLAND

MATIAS GARCIA

BROWNSVILLE RD.

Rachal's Pasture

W.G. COLLINS

AGUA DULCE CRK.

M.Kenedy's Pasture

BLAS MARIA FALCON

LAGUNA LARGO

R.King's Pasture

LAGUNA MADRE

PADRE ISLAND

Gulf of MEXICO

JOHN McCLEAN

M.KENEDY

P.M.DIMOND

ANDRES TREVIÑO

LEONARDO LONGORIA de la GARZA

BERNARDO GARCIA

VICENTE HINOJOSA

MANUEL RAMIREZ ELIZENDO

Filed for record this eleventh day of June 1879

Patrick McDonough
Clerk County Court
Nueces County

Alazan Bay

Salt Lagoon

This map of Nueces County was surveyed by Lafayette Caldwell and adopted by the County Commissioners Court in 1879. It shows some of the larger ranches and original Spanish land grants. The Blas Maria Falcon grant on Agua Dulce Creek was made to a descendant of the first man to establish a settlement in Nueces County. The Corpus Christi and San Diego Railroad (later the Tex-Mex) had only reached as far as Rabb's Pasture at this time.

Caller-Times Archives

c. 1875

Richard King, an orphan in New York, stowed away on a ship bound for Mobile. He worked on riverboats in Alabama and Florida, where he met Mifflin Kenedy. The two men became partners in operating steamboats on the Rio Grande before King established King Ranch in 1853. He was the top taxpayer in Nueces County and the most influential man in the Corpus Christi area before his death in 1885.

Caller-Times Archives

c. 1875

Mifflin Kenedy left Pennsylvania to become a cabin boy on a ship. He later became a riverboat pilot in Florida, where he met another former cabin boy, Richard King. The two came to South Texas to operate steamboats on the Rio Grande. Kenedy joined King in establishing a ranching empire.

Caller-Times Archives

Corpus Christi's Edmund J. Davis had a stormy reign as governor, from 1870 to 1874, in the bitter Reconstruction era. Ex-Confederates hated Davis, but Corpus Christi people remembered his kindness and compassion during the yellow fever epidemic of 1867.

Corpus Christi Central Library

1876
Charles Blucher (top row, far right) was in charge of a surveying expedition. Charles' father, Felix, was Nueces County's first surveyor and Charles followed in the profession. This party included (top row) chain-carriers Richard Blucher and Grove Crafts; and Charles; (bottom row) rodman George Blucher, Philip Fullerton, a guest, and Hilario Martinez, who was in charge of the horses. Richard and George were Charles' brothers.

Chaparral Street, c. 1880
Young girls ride past the
Doddridge & Davis Bank.
The first bicycles arrived in
Corpus Christi in 1869.

Murphy Givens Collection

Louis de Planque/Corpus Christi Central Library

c. 1880

Thomas Beynon, who commanded a cavalry unit in the Confederate army, made a noted ride of 21 miles to come to Corpus Christi's rescue when the town was bombarded by Union naval forces in 1862. Beynon later served as sheriff, owned a livery stable, and ran a stagecoach line to Brownsville. His daughter Sarah married rancher John Wade.

Louis de Planque/Corpus Christi Central Library

c. 1880

Amanda Allen was among those captured in the 1875 raid on Nuecestown, a former river town 12 miles from Corpus Christi, near today's Calallen. The bandits kidnapped people on the roads near Nuecestown. They hanged a man, plundered goods, and set the Noakes store on fire. The captives were freed when the bandits retreated. Texas Rangers under the command of Capt. Leander McNelly were sent to deal with the bandits.

c. 1880

Perry Doddridge, an Alabama orphan, became a successful businessman in Corpus Christi in the 1860s. He and A.M. Davis opened the Doddridge & Davis Bank on Chaparral in 1871. Doddridge served as mayor and county commissioner. He was married to Rachel Lewis Fullerton.

Corpus Christi Central Library

c. 1880

Mauricia Arocha, a native of Mexico, married Frederick Belden in Matamoros and they moved to Corpus Christi in the early 1840s. Belden, a merchant, served on Nueces County's first commissioners court. Zachary Taylor once was a dinner guest at the Belden home at Mesquite and Laguna. The general said his plans were to march to Mexico City. Mauricia Belden said he would never get there. Two years later, Taylor sent Mrs. Belden a silk dress — from Mexico City.

Louis de Planque/Corpus Christi Central Library

c. 1880

John W. Fogg, born in Salem, N.J., owned a livery stable and saloon on Mesquite Street, beginning in the 1860s. He also operated a stagecoach line.

Corpus Christi Central Library

c. 1890s

Charcoal vendors were a common sight on Corpus Christi streets. Housewives used the charcoal for cooking and to heat irons.

c. 1880

Juan Gonzales, born in El Ferrol, Galicia, Spain, in 1835, settled in Corpus Christi in the 1870s. He was a prominent merchant. He died in 1885 and was buried in Holy Cross Cemetery.

c. 1880

Dr. A.G. Heaney moved his family to Corpus Christi from Thomaston, Conn., and began practicing medicine in 1884. He admitted the first patient to Spohn Sanitarium when it opened its doors in 1905. Dr. Heaney owned the city's first telephone company in 1892; his phone number was 1.

Louis de Planque/Corpus Central Library

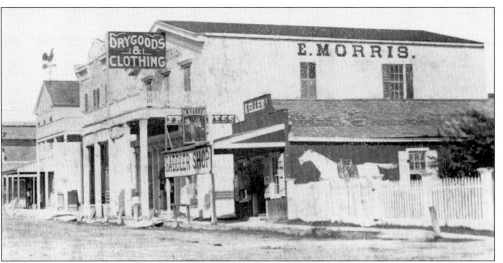

Caller-Times Archives

Chaparral Street, c. 1890

At the corner of Schatzel is Keller's Saddlery, with a white horse painted on its wall, followed by E. Morris' drygoods store, and Norwick Gussett's hide warehouse, with a rooster weathervane.

Caller-Times Archives

May, 1890

The daughters of Charles Carroll, who built St. Patrick's Cathedral in Corpus Christi. Mary Carroll (left, at 6 years old) became a teacher, principal and school superintendent in Corpus Christi; Mary Carroll High is named for her. Mary's sister Lettie Helen (1 year old here) taught ballet in Mexico City for 50 years. Katherine (top) was the mother of Charles Taylor, a Navy pilot who led the flight of five torpedo bombers that disappeared in the Bermuda Triangle on Dec. 5, 1945. The other Carroll sister is Margaret (right).

Upper Broadway, c. 1890

Before it was built, in 1867, lumber for this new Presbyterian Church was stacked on the bluff on a site donated by rancher Richard King when Corpus Christi was hit by a yellow fever epidemic. Hundreds of people were struck down by the fever. The dressed lumber for the church was used to make coffins.

FRANK LESLIE'S ILLUSTRATED NEWSPAPER.

Caller-Times Archives

Sketch of the Alta Vista
Hotel in Corpus Christi
ran in the Oct. 20, 1890,
edition of Leslie's
Weekly.

Caller-Times Archives

1890

Corpus Christi's first major
resort hotel — the Alta Vista
— was patterned after a hotel
in California. It was built in
1890 on a point three miles
south of town (today's Ocean
Drive) by promoter E.H.
Ropes. After Ropes went
bankrupt, the hotel remained
unfinished. It burned in 1927.

c. 1890

Bridget Rosalie Hart came to Texas with her mother in 1832. Rosalie went to a convent school in Mobile where she married John Priour. They returned to Corpus Christi in 1851. Rosalie Priour became a schoolteacher and wrote an autobiography which covers Corpus Christi's grim Civil War years.

Peoples at Mesquite, c. 1890

William Petzel Sr. (center) in front of his meat stall at the old Market Hall.

c. 1890

Thomas B. Southgate came to Corpus Christi from Kentucky in 1881. He was postmaster from 1888 to 1892 and founded the Myrtle Club for men. He started the city's first building and loan society.

Caller-Times Archives

Mesquite Street, c. 1890s

Market Hall was built in 1871 on Market Square, a triangular block bordered by Peoples, Schatzel and Mesquite. The building was financed by private builders who leased stalls to vendors on the lower level. City offices and volunteer firemen occupied space on the second floor. A large dance hall was also on the second floor. Market Hall was torn down in 1911 to make way for a new three-story City Hall built on the site.

Caller-Times Archives

Water Street, c. 1890

Real estate agent E.B. Cole, in the driver's seat, shows a house to prospective buyers. He later donated land for Cole Park.

Caller-Times Archives

Chaparral at Peoples, 1890

Mule teams pull wagons loaded with iron casing for use in artesian wells on the King Ranch. The drilling of artesian wells became widespread in the 1890s. It was a major development in South Texas, giving ranches a dependable source of water. The big building in the center is the E.H. Caldwell Hardware Store.

Caller-Times Archives

Water Street, c. 1890

John Anderson, a sea captain, built a shellcrete home (right) on the waterfront in Corpus Christi in 1851. He built a Dutch-style windmill next to his home after the Civil War.

Mesquite Street, 1895

Mrs. Armstrong's Sunday school class at the First Methodist Church.

First United Methodist Church Archives

Corpus Christi Museum of Science and History

Mestina at Sam Rankin, c. 1895

Water carriers — "barrileros" — wait their turn to fill up with the city's new drinking water, piped in from the Nueces River. Before that, residents relied on cisterns that captured rainwater runoff. The barrileros used 55-gallon barrels on two-wheel carts, which were usually pulled by mules or donkeys.

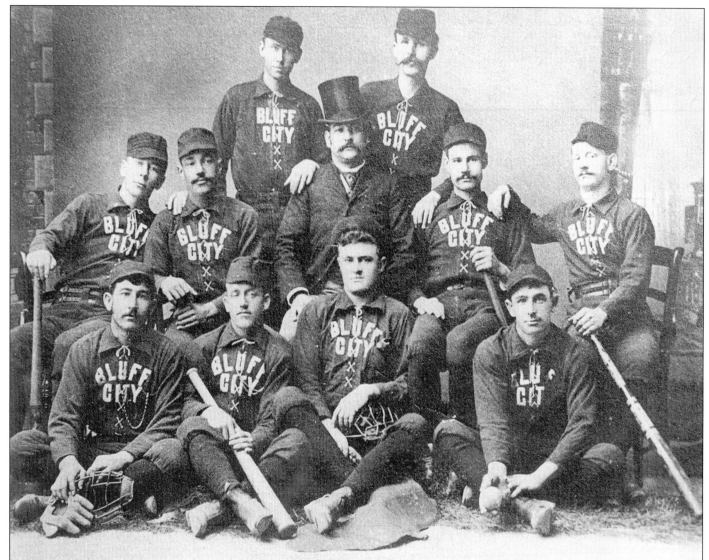

c. 1890
Corpus Christi Bluff City baseball team. The first game was played in the city in 1876. Besides Bluff City, other teams shortly before and after the turn of the century were the Corpus Christi Browns and the Corpus Christi Kids. They played teams from Laredo, San Antonio and Houston. The ballpark was located on Chaparral at Fitzgerald (near today's Heritage Park).

Caller-Times Archives

Caller-Times Archives

1896

Some members of the high school graduating class of 1896 were George Clark, Rayburn Savage, Alice Ricklefsen, Carrie Weil, Edith Evans and Bertha Kaler, among others. Standing in the doorway is principal M. Menger, for whom Menger Elementary was named.

Caller-Times Archives

Mesquite Street, c. 1895

Looking south, Henry Uehlinger's bakery is on the bottom right and the gallery of the Bidwell Hotel is across the street.

**Chaparral Street,
c. 1900**

On Columbus Day, a float
representing one of
Columbus' ships makes
its way past Lichtenstein's
Department Store in the
Uehlinger Building.

Caller-Times Archives

Caller-Times Archives

Mesquite Street, c. 1900

People fill containers with mineral water at Artesian Park. Zachary Taylor's soldiers dug the artesian well in 1845, but the water was too brackish to drink. The well was re-opened in the 1880s and the water became a health tonic. The sign warns that people who bathe or wash animals in the iron tank will be fined.

Caller-Times Archives

Below the bluff, 1898

The Kenedy Rifles, Corpus Christi volunteers for the Spanish-American War, march toward the San Antonio and Aransas Pass Railroad Depot on Belden Street. The Kenedy Rifles missed the fighting, but did garrison duty in Cuba.

Caller-Times Archives

Mesquite Street, 1897
Townspeople threw a few snowballs in front of the Bidwell Hotel during a rare snowstorm in South Texas.

Taylor Street, c. 1900

The Episcopal Church of the Good Shepherd was built at Taylor and Chaparral in 1871. The building was damaged in the 1919 storm and eventually moved to South Staples. A new church was built in 1950.

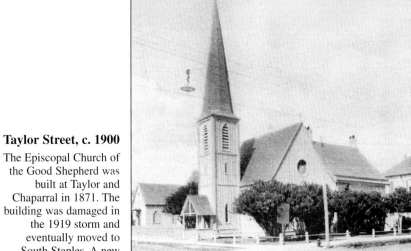

Caller-Times Archives

Caller-Times Archives

c. 1900

Eli Merriman was one of three founders of the *Corpus Christi Caller*, which began publication in 1883. Merriman served as the paper's publisher and editor from its beginning until 1911.

Murphy Givens Collection

Caller-Times Archives

Bayfront, c. 1905

The three-masted schooner Margaret was built on the bayfront in 1905 by Capt. Andy Anderson. The vessel ran onto the rocks near Tampico Bay and smashed to pieces.

Mussett Street, c. 1900

Members of an unidentified African-American family stand by their front gate in Corpus Christi sometime around the turn of the 19th century.

Corpus Christi Central Library

Caller-Times Archives

1901

George Blucher and son take a ride in the family Oldsmobile, shipped in crates from Detroit in October 1901. This is believed to have been the first automobile in Corpus Christi.

Bayfront, 1906

The three-masted schooner Flour Bluff was built in 1860 by Capt. John Anderson. It was constructed with lee boards instead of center boards and made to sail on the shallow waters of Corpus Christi Bay and Laguna Madre. The ship sank in the 1919 storm and was never found.

Caller-Times Archives

Mesquite Street, 1907

The staff of Corpus Christi's *Daily Herald*, with delivery boys in front. The star reporter was the third man from the right, back row, with a droopy mustache, known as "Weary Willie" Waterhouse.

Caller-Times Archives

Mesquite Street, 1907

Pitts Livery sold automobiles, stabled horses and conducted funerals. It was owned by B.H. Pitts and C.P. Baker.

Mesquite at Peoples, 1908

R.G. Blossman and his partner James Thompson were among the city's leading grocers from the 19th into the 20th century. Blossman's had a large wagon yard behind the store for convenient parking for customers.

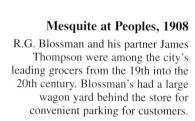

Corpus Christi Central Library

Caller-Times Archives

Mesquite Street, 1907

The Corpus Christi Steam Laundry & Dye Works, at Mesquite and Cooper's Alley, was owned by John Selvidge.

Caller-Times Archives

Corpus Christi Central Library

c. 1910

Ella Barnes, an 18-year-old student at Flour Bluff, was pressed into service to replace a teacher. She taught several years at Flour Bluff and at La Fruta before returning to Corpus Christi in 1899 to join the high school staff. She became the high school principal 23 years later.

Caller-Times Archives

Mesquite Street at Lawrence, c. 1908

The Weil Brothers Grocery opened in 1903 and was run by Alex and Moise Weil until they retired in 1945. Moise Weil (left) is behind the counter and across from him is Joe Mireur, who owned a leather goods store next door.

Mesquite at Peoples, 1909

The Hatch and Robertson building (later called the Lovenskiold Building) housed Bluntzer, Robertson & Co., which sold farm implements. This building still stands on the northwest corner of Mesquite and Peoples.

Corpus Christi Central Library

Corpus Christi Central Library

Mesquite Street, 1909

President William Howard Taft came to South Texas in October, 1909, to visit the Taft Ranch, owned by his half-brother Charles. He came to Corpus Christi on Oct. 22 and spoke from a stand built on the side of the bluff. After the speech, Taft dined at Henrietta King's mansion on the bluff.

c. 1910

S. L. Kostoryz founded the Kostoryz community outside Corpus Christi. He emigrated from Czechoslovakia and settled in Nebraska, where he published a Czech-language newspaper. He sold the paper in 1904 and used the profits to buy 8,000 acres of the Grim Ranch, west of Corpus Christi. He sold farmland to Czech immigrants. He returned to Czechoslovakia in 1920.

Off bayfront, c. 1910

Prospective homebuyers brought here by George H. Paul were given an excursion on the bay in Capt. Andy Anderson's boat Gipsy. The boat was destroyed in the 1919 storm.

Photo Courtesy of Charles L. Baskin

Caller-Times Archives

Bayfront, 1908 and c. 1910

Water slide known as "Old Nat" was located next to George Washington Grim's Natatorium on the bayfront, at the foot of Twigg Street. The windmill pulled up water to keep the slide wet. In the bottom photo, taken about 1910, the windmill and upper structure have been blown away in a storm.

Family photo/Caller-Times Archives

North Broadway, c. 1910

Corpus Christi's most famous physician, Dr. Arthur E. Spohn, sits in his new Cadillac with a niece from Brownsville. Dr. Spohn came to Corpus Christi in 1868, the year after a yellow fever outbreak, as a military quarantine officer. He returned later to marry Sarah Josephine Kenedy, daughter of rancher Mifflin Kenedy.

Caller-Times Archives

North Beach, c. 1910

The first Spohn Hospital was a two-story frame building erected in 1905 on North Beach. It was named in honor of Dr. Arthur Spohn. The hurricane of 1919 washed away much of the building, leaving only the chapel and the south wing.

Caller-Times File Photo

Bayfront, c. 1910

The Pavilion Hotel pier leads to Taylor Street. On the right is the Seaside Hotel, famous for its patio shaded by salt cedars.

Caller-Times Archives

Bayfront, c. 1910

The Pavilion Hotel was built in 1909 by oilman Jack Ennis, who also owned the Seaside Hotel. The hotel, with a dance hall and carnival-like atmosphere, became a favorite entertainment place for Corpus Christi. Rooms in 1910 cost 75 cents a day.

A tip for "Old Jack"

Jack Ennis, the wealthy owner of the Seaside Hotel, was sweeping the cement floor under the salt cedars one day. A woman guest who thought he was one of the hotel's janitors asked him how much he earned. He took his pipe out and said, "Oh, about enough to keep me in tobacco." She reached in her purse and took out two dollars and told him to buy something for himself. He said nothing about owning the hotel, but when she checked out, she discovered her bill had been taken care of by the owner. Ennis told her that, "No woman as kind-hearted as you will have to pay a cent at my hotel."

Family photo/Caller-Times Archives

1910
Mr. and Mrs. Rafael H. Garcia pose on their wedding day on June 4 after the ceremony at St. Patrick's Cathedral by the Rev. Claude Jaillet. Rafael Garcia retired after 50 years as a salesman at Lichtenstein's.

Caller-Times Archives

Caller-Times Archives

Schatzel Street, 1912

Corpus Christi's police department had foot patrolmen wearing London bobby-type helmets while those in the horse patrol wore cavalry hats. The chief of police (seated) was B.C. Baldwin. At left were officers John McMannigal and Stuart Terrell. Others are not identified.

North Beach, 1913

Pilot Charles de Remer (left), W.G. Blake, president of the Commercial Club, postmaster E.G. Crabbe, and *Caller* editor Eli Merriman. De Remer attempted to deliver mail from Corpus Christi to Port Aransas; this was five years before national air-mail service began. Mechanical trouble forced the pilot to return to North Beach. The mail was delivered by boat.

Mesquite Street, c. 1910

The Donigan Building, erected in 1907, leased office space on the ground floor, but most of the three floors were occupied by the State Hotel. The State, built by V.M. Donigan, was Corpus Christi's first modern hotel, with private bathrooms.

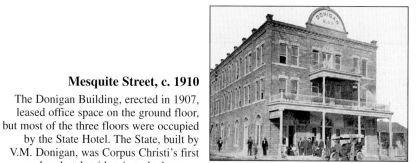

Caller-Times Archives

Caller-Times Archives

Chaparral Street, c. 1910

A streetcar makes its way past the Steen Hotel. Daniel Hewett began the Corpus Christi and Interurban Railway Co. in 1910.

Caller-Times Archives

Corpus Christi Museum

Leopard Street at Artesian, 1914

The American Bottling Co. began in the early part of the century when S.W. Dunnam Sr. bottled and sold fruit juices. He obtained the Coca-Cola franchise for Corpus Christi in 1908. Bottling equipment in 1914 was hand-and-foot-powered. It was said that one employee could bottle 200 cases in 10 hours.

Nueces Bay Causeway, c. 1915

The first causeway across Nueces Bay was built of concrete forms filled with mesquite brush. It had a small lift segment for boat traffic. On the right is a passenger train heading for Corpus Christi on the San Antonio and Aransas Pass trestle. The causeway was damaged in the 1916 hurricane, then destroyed by the 1919 storm.

Waterfront, 1913

The John Dix home, built about 1850, was enlarged and converted into the Seaside Hotel before the turn of the century.

Caller-Times Archives

Caller-Times Archives

Staples Street, c. 1915

Jose J. Gonzalez built this structure in 1911. He operated a furniture store and a theater on the second floor until the building was damaged in the 1919 storm.

Camp Scurry, 1916

Soldiers march down Third Street near Camp Scurry, a base built in what would become the Del Mar neighborhood. After the U.S. entered World War I, the Fifth Engineers and Fourth Field Artillery of the U.S. Army trained at Scurry.

A stylish commemorative plate
of the Seaside Pavilion Hotel
was designed by John T.
McCutcheon.

Bayfront, 1916

Only pilings remain of the wide Pavilion Hotel pier the day after a hurricane made landfall near Corpus Christi. The Pavilion Hotel was one of the few structures on the water to survive the storm, which struck on Friday evening, Aug. 18. It washed away Loyd's Pavilion and Pleasure Pier, the Ladies Pavilion and the Natatorium. It was a prelude to a worst disaster ahead, the storm of 1919.

Caller-Times Archives

Laguna at Mesquite, 1919

Five days after the worst hurricane in Corpus Christi's history struck, a trolley car lies stranded and men load debris on a flatbed truck.

Caller-Times Archives

North Beach, 1919

The morning after the storm, tide waters stood four to six feet high at the U.S. Public Health Service convalescent center, formerly the Breakers Hotel. It was leased by the government to use as a rest home for soldiers wounded in World War I. At the height of the storm, North Beach was covered with 10 to 14 feet of water. Soldiers inside were safe, but many of those who ventured out to try to rescue people clinging to doors, cotton bales, even telephone poles, were lost.

The Storm of 1919

The tropical storm formed near the Windward Islands in the Atlantic. It hit the Florida Keys on Sept. 8, and moved into the Gulf. Storm flags were raised, but Corpus Christi wasn't worried — it had weathered a vicious storm three years before. It started to rain Saturday night. The wind picked up Sunday and by noon it was at gale force, pushing a wall of water before it. Timber from docks and warehouses sliced through the air. North Beach was marooned, then submerged. The wind roared and the water crashed into buildings with incredible force. Hundreds of people were washed out to sea; some estimates placed the death toll at 600.

North Beach was almost swept clear of buildings. Below the bluff, Corpus Christi was a shambles — the streets littered with muck from the bay bottom, cotton bales from the cotton compress, and the smashed detritus of what had been stores and homes. That was the hurricane of 1919, the worst storm in Corpus Christi's history.

Caller-Times Archives

Peoples Street, 1919
By 5 p.m. on Sept. 14, the storm-pushed waters had reached five feet in the downtown area below the bluff.

Chaparral Street, 1919

Looking north down Chaparral, in the aftermath of the storm, the St. James Hotel is surrounded by debris.

Caller-Times Archives

Bayfront, 1919

Looking north, with Chaparral on the left, Corpus Christi below the bluff was badly damaged in the killer storm.

Caller-Times Archives

Mesquite Street, 1919
Looking north from the courthouse to the intersection of Mesquite and Belden in the aftermath of the 1919 storm. The two-story structure in the upper left is the Belden Hotel.

Caller-Times Archives

Bayfront, 1919

A sea of debris awaits clean-up crews after the storm. National Guardsmen were brought in to assist the clean-up and to guard the city from looting. A few days after the storm, the littered area (far left) is where the Convention Center area is today, with Water Street (right) leading south, toward the downtown.

Nueces Bay, 1919

The force of the tidal wave of the storm twisted the railroad tracks on the trestle across Nueces Bay. Some sections of the causeway look untouched while others were completely swept away.

William Street, 1919

Looking toward the bay, downtown Corpus Christi as it appeared after the 1919 storm.

North Beach, 1919

Judge Henry McDonald's house was one of the few structures that remained standing on North Beach in the wake of the storm of 1919. Low-lying North Beach bore the brunt of the storm's fury. Many of the estimated 600 people who drowned in the storm came from the North Beach area. Their bodies, coated with oil from a ruptured oil tank, were swept across Nueces Bay and washed up at such places as White Point.

Chaparral at Water Street, 1919
Salvage workers face a hard job clearing storm debris at the back of the Central Power & Light building.

Water Street at Laguna

Workers clear up lumber and bales of cotton from a cotton compress — after the 1919 storm.

Caller-Times Archives

Mesquite Street, 1919

Wreckage from the storm covers Mesquite Street near the First Methodist Church (center) at the intersection with Mann Street.

Caller-Times Archives

Mesquite Street, 1919

The Nueces County Courthouse is surrounded by debris after the storm. The courthouse served as a refuge during the storm and as a morgue afterwards. Bodies of storm victims were taken to the basement so that survivors could identify family members.

Caller-Times Archives

Caller-Times Archives

Chaparral Street, 1919

One house weathered the storm relatively intact while neighboring houses were leveled.

Seeds of the Storm

It is well if we never forget the sea did rise up. Perhaps, never again will it lift huge blocks of cement from the Causeway and toss them aside as playthings, sweep North Beach and leave it as a sandy beach. May it never again toss our people into its towering waves, to ride a swishing roller-coaster down into a terrifying debris — filled with bales of cotton, huge pilings, walls of houses, pianos, cats, telephone poles, drums of oil, rag dolls . . . I remember the exotic flowers that bloomed in Corpus Christi after the storm, the seeds carried from some distant land. They marked a birth, a new era. Corpus Christi was never the same after the 1919 storm. It grew determinedly, remade, reborn.

— Sister Mary Xavier,
Convent of the Incarnate Word

Chaparral at Peoples Street, 1919

Looking south from the Nueces Hotel, crews are removing storm debris after the 1919 hurricane. The building on the right corner is the Corpus Christi State National Bank. Across Peoples Street is Eidson's Department Store.

Caller-Times Archives

Caller-Times Archives

Water Street at Taylor, 1919

Little remains of Jack Ennis' famous Seaside Hotel, with its grove of salt cedars, in the wake of the storm.

Carrizo at Lipan, c. 1917

A Mexican-American women's auxiliary of a Corpus Christi chapter of the Woodmen of the World gather at Obreros Hall. Identified in photo are: Virginia Reyes (Galvan) (second row, third from right), Ventura Zamudio Sanchez, Mrs. Mircovich, and Josefa Telles. Beatrice Galvan described this auxiliary as "Woodmen of the World ladies."

c. 1917

Members of the young Mexican-American women's organization Sociedad Concordia gather in Corpus Christi. Identified are Jesefa Tellez (seated at far left) and Virginia Reyes Galvan (seated at far right).

Calallen, 1915

Corpus Christi's first water plant was built next to the Nueces River in 1893. The pump house had two steam-driven piston pumps that could handle 750,000 gallons a day each.

Carrizo at Lipan, c. 1920

Members of several Mexican-American organizations gather in front of Obreros Hall. Groups represented include the Woodmen of the World, the Corpus Christi Mexican Band (also known as the B.G. Rodriguez Band), and Sociedad Concordia.

Caller-Times Archives

Caller-Times Archives

Lawrence Street, c. late 1920s

The St. James Hotel (right) at the corner of Chaparral, was the city's finest hotel when it was built in 1870. For many years, it was managed by William Biggio, a veteran of the Confederate Navy. The hotel was torn down in 1937.

Mesquite Street, c. 1920

At the W.T. Harris Grocery Store were (left to right) B.R. Harris, W.T. Harris, J.F. Goforth (by case of beans), Lubin Harris, L.L. Harris and an unidentified man. The store was operated by the Harris brothers.

Caller-Times Archives

Corpus Christi Cathedral Archives

1923

Monsignor Claude Etienne Martin Loup Jaillet came to Texas from France as a young priest in 1866. The Rev. Jaillet (pronounced GHI-YEA) served as the priest at San Diego for 16 years and then at Corpus Christi's St. Patrick's for more than 40 years. As a young man he rode by horseback to remote South Texas ranches.

John Dunn tract, 1922

The Dunn No. 2 gas well blowout on Nov. 8, 1922. The well in the Saxet Heights area, across Nueces Bay from the White Point field, was Corpus Christi's first gas well. It blew at 5 a.m., spewing mud and rocks and accompanied by a deep rumbling noise.

Photo by Harvey Patterson/Caller-Times Archives

Bayfront, 1924

Corpus Christi's Pleasure Pier, built in 1922, was a great attraction for strollers and fishermen. The pier extended from Peoples Street into the bay. The bay excursion boat Japonica was berthed at the end of the pier.

Caller-Times Archives

**Off bayfront,
c. 1925**

The 98-foot pleasure boat Japonica was bought by Capt. Andy Anderson for $3,000 in 1913. The Japonica burned and sank in 1946.

1924

On Nov. 9 a train called The Blackland Special pulled out of Corpus Christi with 108 farmers, businessmen and civic boosters from Corpus Christi and surrounding towns on board. They all sported identical pearl gray Stetsons. The group toured North and Central Texas. The train would stop at selected towns and the men would parade through town and rent a theater to show a film called "Land of Plenty" that promoted the "black-land farming" of the Corpus Christi area.

Caller-Times Archives

Chapman Ranch, c. 1925

The biggest event of the year in the 1920s was the annual barbecue at Chapman Ranch. All South Texans were invited to the all-day affair, and many attended. The meal was free, featuring Chapman Ranch beeves selected for the purpose, along with barrels of trimmings. Chapman Ranch began in 1919 when P.A. Chapman, a Waxahachie farmer, used his oil wealth to buy 34,000 acres from King Ranch, 14 miles south of Corpus Christi. Chapman Ranch became one of the world's earliest mechanized farms.

c. 1925

Ben Garza, a Corpus Christi restaurant owner, was the driving force behind the creation of the League of United Latin American Citizens, a national civil rights organization formed in Corpus Christi in 1929. Garza was elected its first president. He died in 1937.

Caller-Times Archives

Caller-Times Archives

North Mesquite, c. 1925

This building at the corner of Mesquite and Mann, built in 1912, was the third home of the First Methodist Church. When the church was under construction, Rev. T. F. Sessions would give the workers "faith checks" on Saturday and church elders would go to the bank on Monday and sign personal notes to cover the checks. The building was torn down after a new church was built on Shoreline in 1955.

Caller-Times Archives

Starr Street, 1924

Mail carriers in the Corpus Christi Postal Department gather outside the federal building. The postmaster was Owen D. Holleman, shown at far left. Others (standing, left to right) were: Charles Kaler, J.F. Herold, R.L. Harrell, J.B. Pitman, E.T. Cox, Cyrus Tillotson, C.B. Kaler, and Hiram Riggs. Seated (left to right) were: F.J. Jenkins, Don Harris, H.J. Stevens, I.C. Kerridge, W.L. DeRoche, and Joe Dunlap.

c. 1925

A returned
hunter's trophies.

Murphy Givens Collection

Shopping at Lichtenstein's

Chaparral at Schatzel, c. 1925

This was Lichtenstein's third store, built in 1911. The new building was ahead of its time in Corpus Christi with modern elevators and a safety sprinkler system. Lichtenstein's moved to its fourth and final location on Chaparral in 1941.

Caller-Times Archives

William Fuller in memoirs about growing up in Corpus Christi — "When the Century and I Were Young" — described visits to Lichtenstein's with his mother.

"Warned from boyhood never to touch anything in a store, I was free to wander. But wander where? My first few minutes were taken up with those noisy mechanical marvels, the baskets running from various points in the store up to the mezzanine. The baskets were made of wire and ran on little cables. Purchases were placed in the baskets along with a little leather cup containing the sales slip and, if a cash sale, the money.

"A lever released a spring which sent the basket flying up to the mezzanine, where goods were wrapped, charges recorded, and change made. Small boys were entranced by the metallic clacks of catches and spring releases at either end, and the whir of the sailing baskets."

Chaparral at Schatzel, 1925

Landmark structures in this shot are the Nueces Hotel (right of the signal) and Lichtenstein's third department store (with awning on the right). Across from Lichtenstein's is the Corpus Christi National Bank.

Caller-Times Archives

Chaparral at Starr, c. 1925

Simon-Cohn department store anchored the northwest end of the 600 block of Chaparral before J.C. Penney acquired this property in the 1930s. The big building on the block is Kress Five-and-Dime, followed by the City National Bank at the corner of Peoples.

Mesquite Street, 1927

Zip Battery Service was owned by Cipriano "Zip" Gonzalez (left). His employees, by their service vehicles, included (left to right) Willie Jordan, C. Trevino, Bob Williams and Walter Lawrence.

Peoples at Chaparral, c. 1925

The City National Bank was established in 1904 by Clark Pease.

Lawrence at Mesquite, 1927

Looking toward the bay, the building at left is the Bidwell Hotel, built in 1890 as the Constantine Hotel. What was left of the Bidwell was torn down in 1999.

First United Methodist Church Archives

North Mesquite, c. 1925

The orchestra of the First Methodist Church, under the direction of J. Ivy McClain (lower left, holding a violin), played for general assemblies on Sunday mornings and gave a monthly concert at evening services during its heyday between 1924 and 1928.

Third Street at Ayers, 1925

After Spohn Hospital on North Beach was all but destroyed in the 1919 storm, Henrietta King donated five acres along the bay as a place for a new hospital site. Many considered it too far outside the city limits to be a suitable location, but the new Spohn Hospital was built on the site, where it is still located.

Caller-Times Archives

Caller-Times Archives

Mesquite Street, 1926

Sailors march down Mesquite, past the Lovenskiold Building, Nau Hardware, and Harris Grocery in the port dedication day parade. The parade culminated at Cargo Dock No. 1, where a large crowd gathered to watch the first vessels enter the new Port of Corpus Christi.

Caller-Times Archives

The official program brochure for port opening day on Sept. 14, 1926. Activities included a parade, dedication ceremonies, motorboat races, a beauty contest and a historical pageant. The city spent more than $50,000 on the celebration.

Port Opening Day

Sept. 14, 1926, was the biggest celebration in Corpus Christi's history. Special trains brought visitors from Laredo, Houston and San Antonio. Excursion boats arrived from Galveston and Beaumont. Some 25,000 visitors arrived to help celebrate the occasion. The U.S. Navy sent three destroyers. A parade through the downtown area ended up at Cargo Dock No. 1. Sirens blew, flags waved and people cheered. A favorite attraction was the new bascule bridge. Speakers were former Gov. Pat Neff, Congressman John Nance Garner, and Roy Miller, the former *Caller* publisher and Corpus Christi mayor who lobbied Congress for the port authorization funding.

The dedication of the new port was on the seventh anniversary of the great hurricane of 1919. Following that disaster, Corpus Christi had vowed to come back, and its citizens worked to gain federal authorization for the new ship channel and port. On port opening day, it was understood that the future growth of Corpus Christi would depend on the success of the new port.

Caller-Times Archives

Port area, 1926
People watch the freighter Ogontz move through the bascule bridge channel into the new port turning basin.

Caller-Times Archives

Port, 1926
The Col. Keith, an ocean-going barge, was the first commercial vessel to enter the new Port of Corpus Christi on port opening day.

Doc McGregor/Caller-Times Archives

Caller-Times Archives

North Beach, 1930

An old three-masted sailing ship was moved to North Beach in 1927 and was sunk in the sand beside a pier. Simply called "The Ship," it became a popular place where couples could dance on the waterfront. It almost came to disaster in 1932 when the USS Constitution, "Old Ironsides," visited Corpus Christi. The wake from two destroyers escorting the frigate raised The Ship off its sand base and it tore loose from its moorings. After much difficulty, it was moved back to its former location. The Ship was sold for salvage after it was damaged in the 1933 storm.

North Chaparral, 1927

At the Nueces Shoe Repairing Company, customers could have their shoes resoled and shined, their hats blocked, their suits pressed, and they could even take a hot or cold bath. Owners were Jim Dimotsis and George Strates.

North Staples, 1928

The wedding guests of Beatrice Galvan and Joe De La Vina gather outside the Galvan home on Jan. 1. Identified are: George Schunior Jr., Juan De La Vina, Juan Galvan Jr., Gabe Lozano, Salvador Cardenas, Lupe Curiel, Jose Barrera Guerra, Andres Chavez, Raymond Benson, Joe Garza, Willie Benson, Beto Reyna, Ben Garza Sr., Joe De La Vina, Beatrice Galvan, Mrs. Ben Garza, Alma Botello, Mrs. Willie Benson, Irene De La Vina, Ofelia Muguerza, Maria Quiroz, Rosa Chapa Lozano, Nieves Olivares, Elvira Reyna, Celia Lozano, Paula Lozano, Estella Olivarez, Rosa Galvan, Ben Garza Jr., Mary Garza, Ernestina De La Vina, Ernestina Lozano, Patty Galvan, and Mamie Galvan. Others were not identified.

Corpus Christi Central Library

Mesquite Street, 1929

The Order of Sons of America, a fraternal and patriotic group, was a forerunner of the League of United Latin American Citizens. This photo was taken on the steps of the Methodist Church in 1929, before the meeting in May when LULAC was formed. On the front row (left of the sailor by the flag) is Ben Garza, who owned the Metropolitan Café and became LULAC's first president. Many of the members of this organization became founding members of LULAC.

Caller-Times Archives

1929

Delegates at the first convention of the League of United Latin American Citizens (LULAC) gather at the bluff balustrade in Corpus Christi in May, 1929. Earlier that year, in February at Obreros Hall, Corpus Christi's Ben Garza was instrumental in getting three Hispanic civil rights organizations in South Texas to combine into one organization — LULAC. At the first convention, Garza was elected president and Luis Wilmot, also of Corpus Christi, was elected treasurer. Garza, holding a hat, is in the middle of the front row, fifth from left.

Caller-Times Archives

Leopard Street, c. 1930

The Nueces Drug Store on the left was eventually replaced by DeLeon Pharmacy. Down the block is the Melba Theater and across the street is the Grande. At the end of Leopard is the White Plaza Hotel and the Nixon Building.

c. 1930

Officers of the
Corpus Christi
Mexican-American
women's
organization
"Leona Vilario" of
the Obreros
y Obreras.

Flour Bluff, c. 1931

Returning from a trip to Padre Island on the Don Patricio Causeway were (left, on car running board) Evelyn Buckley Maurin and Annie Oliver Green. Girls were (left to right) Mary Ann Buckley Rachal, 7; girl with her head down unidentified; and Hannah Green Haegelin, 10.

Caller-Times Archives

Padre Island, c. 1930

Men hoist a car back on the troughs on the Don Patricio Causeway. This was a common occurrence since it was easy for an inattentive driver to get out of the narrow wooden ruts. It was said that three trips on the causeway would ruin a set of tires from the planks rubbing against them.

Doc McGregor Photo Collection/Corpus Christi Museum of Science and History

Leopard Street, 1931

Leopard Street was Corpus Christi's busiest thoroughfare when this photo was taken on Aug. 29, 1931.

Doc McGregor Photo Collection/Corpus Christi Museum of Science and History

Mesquite Street, 1930

Looking north, toward the First Methodist Church with its rounded dome, the old State Hotel (left) dominates the 700 block of Mesquite. On the right is the Ritz Theater, which stretched between Chaparral and Mesquite.

Doc McGregor Photo Collection/Corpus Christi Museum of Science and History

Photo by Doc McGregor

Municipal Airport, 1932

An American Airways flight from Brownsville on June 1 inaugurates air-mail service for Corpus Christi. When the 10-passenger Fairchild took off for San Antonio, it was carrying 360 pounds of U.S. mail.

Doc McGregor/Caller-Times Archives

Bayfront, 1932

John Govatos' Pier Café, which anchored the land side of the Pleasure Pier, was one of Corpus Christi's most popular restaurants. It was started in 1926 in a remodeled fishing shack on the waterfront; a new building was erected in 1932. The Pier Cafe was closed in 1942 after it was left high and dry on Water Street after the seawall was built.

Doc McGregor/Corpus Christi Museum of Science and History

Bayfront, 1932

Tugs move the USS Constitution through the narrow bascule bridge opening. During its nine-stay at the port in February, 1932, the old frigate was visited by an estimated 100,000 people. The Constitution gained fame in the War of 1812; Oliver Wendell Holmes wrote the ballad "Old Ironsides" when the Navy planned to scrap her after the war. "Old Ironsides" lost a little wood when the ship scraped the side of the bascule bridge entrance.

Third Street, 1932

Police officers raided a home and confiscated a still used to make rye whiskey in the year before Prohibition was repealed. Leading the raid was Ike Elliff (left) and officer Frank Krees; the third man was Clark Aten, a reporter for the *Corpus Christi Times*, and officer Andrew Alvarez.

Doc McGregor/Corpus Christi Museum of Science and History

Caller-Times Archives

Industrializing the Port

The Coastal Bend economy in 1933 was based on agriculture, mostly cotton. That began to change when a company known as Southern Alkali (later Pittsburgh Plate Glass) established the first major industrial plant here. Its purpose was to produce chlorine and soda ash, using oyster shells as the raw material.

One immediate result was to provide desperately needed jobs during the dark days of the Great Depression.

Another result was longer lasting. The port, to accommodate the needs of this new plant, made improvements which attracted other industries.

This started a chain reaction that eventually brought refineries and chemical plants to Corpus Christi.

1933
In the depths of the Great Depression, men in Corpus Christi wait to apply for work building a plant to produce chlorine and soda ash. Southern Alkali was the first major industrial concern to locate in Corpus Christi.

**Port of
Corpus Christi, 1935**

The Bull Steamship
Lines' Dorothy unloads
a cargo of trucks at
the port.

Caller-Times Archives

Doc McGregor/Corpus Christi Museum of Science and History

North Beach, 1934

Destroyed by the 1919 storm, North Beach made its way back in the 1920s and '30s to become a favorite playground for South Texas. North Beach began to decline after the Padre Island Causeway was opened in 1950.

Pleasure Pier, 1934

The city's Pleasure Pier attracted strollers and fishermen before the seawall, L-head and T-heads were built six years later.

Caller-Times Archives

Caller Times Archives

Schatzel Street, 1934

Sixteen members of Corpus Christi's 20-man police department include (standing, left to right): Dan Sullivan, George Lowman, Wilbur Dugat, John Gane, Lee Petzel, Pop Watkins, Joe Rackley, Lloyd Magee, Ed Flint, Slim Adkinson, Joe Davis, Henry Cobb and Peter Tunchez. Seated were N.D. Huey, assistant chief, Albert Mace, chief of police, and Pop Horn, dispatcher.

Caller-Times Archives

Water Street, 1935

The Princess Louise Hotel, which opened in 1928, became the city's most fashionable resort hotel. At high tide, the waters from Corpus Christi Bay lapped at the foot of the fountain in the Princess Louise patio.

Water Street at Mann, c. 1940

The Princess Louise Hotel opened in January, 1928. The 110-room pink stucco hotel, with its red-tile roof, became one of the city's most recognizable landmarks on the waterfront. The hotel was built by Mrs. Walter Foster and her brother John F. Saunders after the Chamber of Commerce put up a $10,000 bonus to any developer who would build a resort hotel on the bayfront. The hotel was remodeled in the 1960s into an apartment complex.

Caller-Times Archives

Upper Broadway, 1935

The Nixon Building (left) and the Plaza Hotel (right) were the tallest buildings in the city in the 1930s. The Nixon Building (later the Wilson Building) housed many of the offices of the principal oil companies. The lobby of the Plaza was a favorite meeting place of oilmen.

Doc McGregor Photo Collection/Corpus Christi Museum of Science and History

Doc McGregor/Caller-Times Archives

Up River Road, 1936

"Red" John Dunn stands in front of his museum, which contained one of the largest privately owned collections of historical artifacts in the country. He gathered firearms and weapons of all nations, including guns captured from South Texas bandits when he was a Texas Ranger. Dunn's memoirs titled "Perilous Trails of Texas," written after he was 80 years old, recounts bandit raids and pioneer days in old Corpus Christi.

Bayfront, 1935

With the bay in the background, Capt. Andy Anderson shows off a model of the schooner Petrel that he built. Anderson, his father John and brother William were longtime boat owners and bay pilots. Andy Anderson owned the schooner Gipsy and the bay pleasure excursion boat Japonica.

Doc McGregor/Caller-Times Archives

Chaparral Street, 1935

On the left is the Rio Theater next to the Mayflower Cafe. Across is the street are Kress and Draughon's Practical Business College.

Caller-Times Archives

South Broadway, 1940

Dr. H.R. Giles, outside his home on South Broadway, practiced medicine in Corpus Christi for 47 years. He was elected mayor in 1935 and served one term.

Doc McGregor/Caller-Times

North Chaparral, 1935

A city bus makes its way south through heavy traffic in this pre-Christmas scene. On the right is the Nueces Shoe Co. and Draughon's Practical Business College, and on the left is the Mayflower Café and J.C. Penney.

Chaparral Street, 1936

A crowd gathers on April 15 at the Palace Theater to see the Major Bowes Talent Show, which was touring nationally. The Palace, built in 1925, burned on Dec. 3, 1953.

Caller-Times Archives

Looking south on Water Street, 1935

The counter-balanced bascule bridge at the entrance to the Port of Corpus Christi was painted black and coated with grease to protect it from the salt air. It was 124 feet long, 52 feet wide, and one end could be raised 141 feet into the air. The bridge could be raised in one minute by two 100-horsepower electric motors.

Water Street, c. 1920s

The bascule bridge, which began operations in 1926, allows a ship to enter the port turning basin; North Beach is on the right. The new bridge (named for "seesaw" in French) was built by the Wisconsin Bridge and Iron Co. It cost $400,000. When raised for ships entering the new port, the bridge stayed up for 20 to 30 minutes or longer, frustrating drivers and holding up commerce. It only took a minute for the massive iron span to open, but it was raised when vessels were still way out in the bay in order to give them time to reverse engines if the bridge mechanism failed.

Carancahua, 1938

St. Patrick's Cathedral, built in 1881 at a cost of $15,000, was damaged in November when a fire broke out in the church's south tower. A fund drive for a new cathedral was started the next day and ground was broken on the site of the new cathedral on March 1, 1939; the building was finished the following year. St. Patrick's was dismantled in 1951 and used as the framework for the church on North Beach, "Our Lady of the Sea."

Corpus Christi Cathedral Archives

Caller-Times Archives

North Chaparral, 1938

Dr. John Frederick McGregor took thousands of photographs of Corpus Christi and its people over a 30-year period. He took many of the photos appearing in this book. His nickname "Doc" came from the fact that he was also a practicing chiropractor.

Doc McGregor/Corpus Christi Museum of Science and History

Nueces County, 1937

Cotton pickers near Corpus Christi. For the 1920s and early '30s, the Corpus Christi economy depended on cotton production, before farmers began to switch to grain sorghum and before the city began to attract port area industries. At cotton-picking time, pickers came here from all over Texas. Downtown around Leopard Street was always crowded on Saturdays when cotton-picking families came to spend their weekly wages.

Russell Lee/Library of Congress

North Beach, 1939

The Rincon Coffee Shop and Grocery, operated by B. H. Browne, catered to people living at the Rincon Trailer Court and several tourist courts.

Russell Lee/Library of Congress

North Beach, 1940

Young woman washes clothes near the family outhouse. She and her family lived in a tent near Rincon Point.

Russell Lee/Library of Congress

North Beach, 1940

A roofer and his daughter in front of their tent home. The man worked at the Naval Air Station, making $1 per hour. There was a critical shortage of housing available in the city because of the influx of workers to build the base. Many of the unskilled and semi-skilled workers and their families lived in shacks and tents in an area of North Beach fronting on Nueces Bay.

Russell Lee/Library of Congress

North Beach, 1940
The interior of a tent occupied by a roofer and his family.

North Beach, 1939
Shack of a World War
I veteran facing
Nueces Bay. This area
became a squatters
camp in 1940 when
unskilled workers
flooded the area
looking for
construction jobs at
the new naval base.

Russell Lee/Library of Congress

Russell Lee/Library of Congress

Corpus Christi, 1940
A construction worker could only find a shack to house his family. Corpus Christi suffered a severe housing shortage with the arrival in the summer of 1940 of some 9,000 workers to build the base.

Russell Lee/Library of Congress

North Beach, 1940

A carpenter's helper and his family live in a trailer. He came to Corpus Christi seeking work at the new naval base.

Russell Lee/Library of Congress

Lower North Broadway, 1940
Men apply at the Texas State Employment Service office for work building the new naval base.

Russell Lee/Library of Congress

North Staples, 1940

Men eat an afternoon meal at the Salvation Army. Although there was a shortage of skilled labor needed to help build the Naval Air Station, many unskilled workers could not find jobs.

Russell Lee/Library of Congress

Lower North Broadway, 1940
A job applicant is interviewed at the Texas State Employment Service office.

"Doc" McGregor/Caller-Times Archives

Bayfront, 1940

The seawall nears completion. Work began early in 1939 on a project that would completely change Corpus Christi's shoreline appearance — a 12,000-foot-long seawall. The seawall was built along a levee that was as much as 100 yards from the old water line off Water Street. Completed in 1941, the stepped seawall and the two T-Heads and L-Head cost $2.2 million. The concrete base in the foreground was the beginning of work for the Lawrence Street T-Head.

Caller-Times Archives

Bayfront, 1941

Construction of the seawall moves toward the south. The odd-looking structure (above, left) was a movable form used to mold the steps of the seawall. It was 40 feet long and progressed its own length each day. The roof gave protection from the sun.

Caller-Times Archives

Bayfront, 1940

The $2 million seawall is under construction by contractor J. DePuy of San Antonio, the firm that also built the breakwater in 1925. The seawall was designed by Myers & Noyes of Dallas, project engineers. Creosoted pilings were driven into the bay base to form braces for the levee. The seawall represented the front of that dirt levee. The cement for the seawall was mixed with bay saltwater rather than the usual freshwater.

Russell Lee/Library of Congress

Bayfront, 1940

Corpus Christi's seawall nears completion at the end of 1940. The new stepped seawall, forming a scenic amphitheater, would prove to be popular with residents and visitors alike.

Flour Bluff, 1940

Construction equipment has begun to arrive for building the Naval Air Station in June 1940. Announcement that a naval base would be located at Corpus Christi was made in the fall of 1939. Work began in the summer of 1940 and thanks to a nine-month frenzy of activity by more than 9,000 workers, the base was 70 percent completed by the time it was dedicated on March 12, 1941.

U.S. Navy Photograph/Caller-Times Archives

Flour Bluff, 1940

An area of sand dunes and brush land by the bay (the old Spanish Rincon de Grulla) was turned into a busy complex of runways, hangars and paved roads that would comprise the Naval Air Station at Corpus Christi. Sand dunes, some as high as 40 feet, were leveled. This area was being graded for seaplane hangars.

Russell Lee/Library of Congress

Flour Bluff, 1940

Truck drivers who work at the new Naval Air Station under construction.

Russell Lee/Library of Congress

Over Flour Bluff, 1940

Aerial view shows completed runways at Corpus Christi Naval Air Station in December, 1940, only nine months after construction began. The base opened for flight training the following March.

U.S. Navy Photograph/Caller-Times Archives

Flour Bluff, 1940

A hod carrier works on a project to build 249 housing units for married personnel at the naval base under construction.

Naval air station, 1941

A sailor walks near Building One, headquarters of Corpus Christi Naval Air Station. Because many took off their shoes to walk through the sand, water faucets and towels were provided at the entrance of buildings so people could wash their feet before putting their shoes and socks back on.

U.S. Navy Photograph/Caller-Times Archives

Flour Bluff, 1940

Buses used to transport civilian construction workers to the Naval Air Station.

Flour Bluff, 1940

A line-up of trucks and their drivers near the Naval Air Station under construction.

Downtown, 1940

A civilian worker at the Naval Air Station wears a badge that allows him to enter the base.

Russell Lee/Library of Congress

Caller-Times Archives

Mesquite Street, 1940

Thomas F. Rape (left), an assistant night jailer at the Nueces County Jail and a veteran of the Spanish-American War, volunteered to serve as a draft registrar on national registration day on Oct. 16. Registering for the draft were Lewis C. Bramlette (center) and David P. Ayers.

Chaparral Street, 1941

A man in front of the Nueces Hotel Coffee Shop buys a *Caller* Extra on Dec. 7 reporting the Japanese attack on Pearl Harbor earlier that day.

Caller-Times Archives

Caller-Times Archives

There Goes Peacetime

Corpus Christi's reaction to the Japanese attack on Pearl Harbor was summed up in the Monday, Dec. 8, edition of the *Caller*: "In Corpus Christi as war struck at Hawaii: The deceptive Sunday calm, with excitement gathering as an undercurrent . . . surprise . . . incredulity . . . and a surprising feeling of relief, for the war of nerves is over and the real thing begins . . . a people tired of appeasement wanting to let 'em have it.

"The radio announcement that the president had ordered defensive plans put in action . . . and a service station attendant asking, 'Are we going to defend or are we going to attack?'

"The *Caller-Times'* phone ringing off the wall . . . people wanting news . . . news . . . what's happening? . . . printers in their Sunday clothes running upstairs to start work on the Extra . . . One man calling in the midst of the furor wanting to know the time . . . the amazement of those who hadn't heard. Calls from persons with relatives in Hawaii . . . a Corpus Christian with a brother in Schofield Barracks . . . another whose father is en route to China . . . white-faced aviation cadets . . . blasé shore patrolmen . . . There goes peacetime."

Starr Street, 1941

After the Japanese attack on Pearl Harbor, local recruiting offices were swamped with volunteers, many of them too old or too young for the military. Before the month of December was out, 135 area men, calling themselves the Avengers of Pearl Harbor, were sworn in in front of the federal building.

NOW PLAYING

Captain Caution

VICTOR MATURE LOUISE PLATT LEO CARRILLO BRUCE CABOT

Also Select SHORT SUBJECTS

Photo by Doc McGregor/Caller-Times Archives

Leopard Street, 1941

Melba Theater employees are dressed as cowgirls for a promotion. The Melba opened in 1926 as the Leopard Theater; the foyer featured a mosaic of a leopard. It was located across the street from another popular theater in the 1930s and '40s, the Grande.

Corpus Christi Central Library

Leopard Street, 1941
Officials of the League of United Latin American Citizens take part in a "Defense Bond Day" parade on Dec. 19, 1941, more than a week after the attack on Pearl Harbor. Some 50 floats took part in the parade to kick off a campaign to sell $1 million in defense savings bonds in Corpus Christi.

Bayfront, 1941

An ill-fated PBY (Patrol Boat, with Y as the manufacturer's classification) plane landed near the T-Head on Jan. 8, 1941. The plane, on a flight from San Diego, Calif., to Pensacola, ran into a West Texas norther, forcing some of the crew to bail out and the pilot who stayed with the plane to detour 500 miles south. One crewman was killed when his parachute failed to open and four others were killed after they were rescued and the Navy transport plane carrying them back to San Diego crashed. After landing on the bay, the pilot and co-pilot flew the plane on to Pensacola.

Caller-Times Archives

Bayfront, 1941

One of the first PBYs used in training at the Corpus Christi Naval Air Station flies over the bay in February. The NAS received its first class of 52 pilot trainees in March. PBYs like this one were a common sight around Corpus Christi during World War II. The PBYs were eventually replaced by the PBM Mariner and then the Marlin.

Naval air station, 1941

Gerald F. Child was one of the first to graduate from flight training at the Naval Air Station. More than a year later, at the Battle of Midway, Child and his PBY crew were the first to locate the Japanese fleet. They kept visual contact for three hours before their plane was shot down by a Japanese fighter. They stayed in the water overnight before being rescued. Child was awarded the Navy Air Medal three times before the war was over.

Caller-Times Archives

Howard Hollem/Library of Congress

Naval air station, 1942

Cadets watch others practice landings. More than 35,000 naval aviators were trained during World War II at Corpus Christi NAS, which played a major role in winning the war in the Pacific.

Howard Hollem/Library of Congress

Naval air station, 1942

Aviation cadets check the flight board before going to their planes. The board showed the plane number, take-off time, and the instructor assigned to each cadet for that day's flights.

U.S. Navy Photograph/Caller-Times Archives

Naval air station, 1941

Lt. E.W. Allen presents "wings" to the first cadets to solo in flight training at the naval air station. Toward the end of 1941, Corpus Christi NAS was turning out 300 aviators each month. After the attack on Pearl Harbor, the number was doubled. Eventually, 35,000 naval aviators were trained at Corpus Christi NAS with its four divisions, including the main base at Flour Bluff and three outlying fields bordering Oso Creek — Rodd, Cabaniss and Cuddihy Fields.

Howard Hollem/Library of Congress

Naval air station, 1942

Jesse Rhodes Waller, aviation ordnance mate, checks out a 30-caliber machine gun he has just installed in a Navy plane.

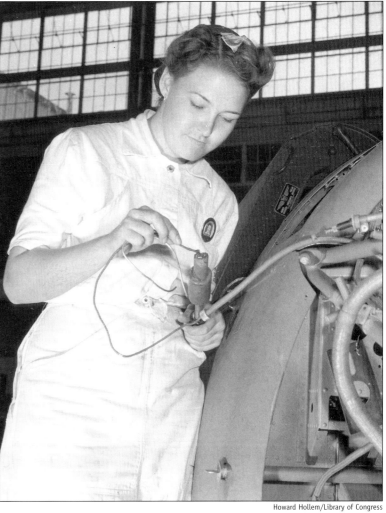

Howard Hollem/Library of Congress

Naval air station, 1942

Jo Ann Whitington, a former telephone operator, learns to solder wires. She was being trained through the National Youth Administration (NYA) program for a civil service job in the Assembly & Repairs Department at the base.

Howard Hollem/Library of Congress

Naval air station, 1942

Irma Lee McElroy, a former office worker, paints insignia on airplane wings.

Howard Hollem/Library of Congress

Naval air station, 1942

Sisters Evelyn and Lillian Buxkeurple work on a practice bomb shell. They volunteered to leave the farm to become trainees for civilian jobs at the naval base.

Howard Hollem/Library of Congress

Naval air station, 1942
Women workers in the Assembly & Repair Department take their lunch break in the shade of a Navy plane. Young women wearing coveralls and carrying lunch pails were a common sight in Corpus Christi during World War II.

Doc McGregor/Caller-Times Archives

North Broadway, 1941

A construction worker at the Robert Driscoll Hotel has a view of the downtown. The hotel opened in May 1942 and closed in 1970. It was renovated in the 1980s to become the First City Bank Building.

PHOTO SERVICE
TOGRAPHERS — KODAK FINISHING

Caller-Times Archives

Upper Broadway, 1942

The Robert Driscoll Hotel nears completion in the spring of '42. The hotel was built by Clara Driscoll and named for her late brother. Rumor had it that she built the hotel because she had a grudge against the White Plaza Hotel next door. Many famous people stayed at the Driscoll in the 1940s, including Mary Pickford, John Wayne and Tyrone Power, who kept a room there while he was in training as a Navy pilot at the Naval Air Station during World War II.

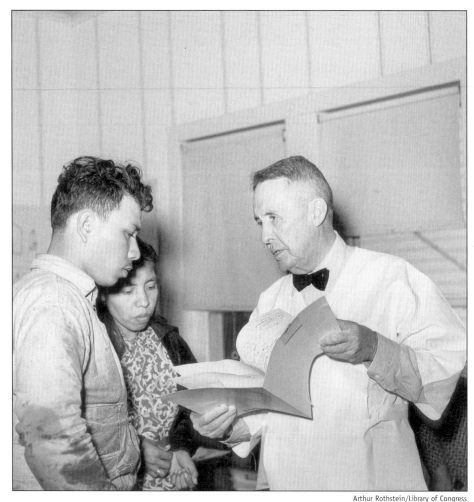

Arthur Rothstein/Library of Congress

1942

The doctor of a privately supported tuberculosis clinic in Corpus Christi discusses treatment with family members of a patient. TB became a major health problem, leading Nueces County to establish the Hilltop Hospital for treating tuberculosis in 1953.

Caller-Times Archives

Calallen, 1953

Nueces County's new tuberculosis hospital opened in February, 1953, where volunteers originally established Hilltop Hospital in 1943. The county took over Hilltop Hospital in 1949 and built a six-wing, $900,000 facility for the treatment of tuberculosis, a major health problem in the 1950s and early 1960s. The old Hilltop facility burned on May 18, 1953. The new hospital soon reached capacity, with more than 100 patients being treated for TB. The hospital was closed in 1967.

1942

Dr. Hector P. Garcia in the U.S. Army. He served as an infantry officer, and then as a doctor in the medical corps. Dr. Garcia returned from the battlefields of Europe after World War II to lead the fight at home to change laws and public opinion to give Mexican-Americans equal rights and equal opportunity.

1958

Dr. Hector P. Garcia (left) shakes hands with an unidentified GI Forum official from Colorado (center) and state Sen. Henry B. Gonzalez of San Antonio at a GI Forum convention.

Belden Street, 1942

When milkmen became scarce during World War II, women were hired to make route deliveries. Elsie Moore was hired by Grisham's Dairy in November 1942 and worked until the end of the war.

North Beach, c. 1942

The North Beach Amusement Park was a crowded place in the 1940s.

Chaparral Street, 1942

Corpus Christi firemen, fire department officials and police officers attend a Palace Theater showing of a movie about Clyde Barrow and Bonnie Parker for a firemen's benefit.

c. 1942
Corpus Christi women register for sugar rationing during World War II.

Photo by Doc McGregor/Caller-Times Archives

North Beach, 1942

A saltwater pool featured piped-in bay water for a protected swim. It was built in 1926 by Bruce L. Collins, who also owned the North Beach Bath House and North Beach Pleasure Park. The saltwater pool was torn down in the late 1950s to make way for what is today the Sandy Shores Hotel.

Caller-Times Archives

Chaparral Street, c. 1942

The Palace on Chaparral, built in 1926, was the city's first major theater. It burned in a spectacular fire in 1953, which provided one last evening's entertainment for the guests of the nearby Nueces Hotel.

Caller-Times Archives

Ayers Street, 1945

Wynn Seale students
dance the jitterbug at a
school dance on Dec. 12.

Caller-Times Archives

Spudder Park, 1946

The Southwest Texas Rodeo kicked off on June 4 at Spudder Park, on the south side of Leopard Street near Port Avenue. The park got its name from a semi-pro baseball team that played there in the 1930s — the Corpus Christi Spudders.

Water Street, 1947

Linn K. "Doc" Mason was the owner and operator of Corpus Christi's swanky nightclub of the 1930s and 1940s, the Dragon Grill, which started in 1930 on North Beach and moved to a new location on North Water Street in 1946. The Dragon Grill was famous for its food, its entertainment, and its illegal gambling. After it was raided in 1953, the Dragon Grill was closed and Mason moved to Las Vegas.

Naval air station, c. 1947

Ralph Galvan's orchestra plays at the CPO Club at NAS Corpus Christi. Shown are (left to right) Ralph Galvan, Eddie Galvan, Buddy Blair, Joe Medina, Billy Davis, Bill Haverfield, and Bobby Galvan.

Caller-Times Archives

Caller-Times Archives

Lyndon and Lady Bird Johnson on a visit to Corpus Christi.

Bayfront, 1948

A helicopter nicknamed "the Johnson City Windmill" prepares to land Senate candidate Lyndon Johnson for a campaign speech in Corpus Christi July 8, 1948. The 'copter put down where Memorial Coliseum is located now.

South Water Street, c. 1949

Zackie's Playhouse was one of two drive-ins owned by Dave Zackie; the second was located where U&I Restaurant is today. Another popular drive-in in the late 1940s was the High Hat, on Staples. Mac's, Pick's, and Snapka's (still in business) were built in the 1950s.

Artesian Park, 1948

Domino players concentrate on the game on a fine October day.

Caller-Times Archives

Roy Miller makes a campaign speech for "Cactus Jack" Garner. Miller came to Corpus Christi in 1904 as a railroad publicity agent. He became editor of the *Caller* three years later and was elected mayor in 1913, at age 29. He went to Washington to lobby for a deepwater port in 1922. He died in 1946 and Corpus Christi High School was renamed Roy Miller High School in his honor.

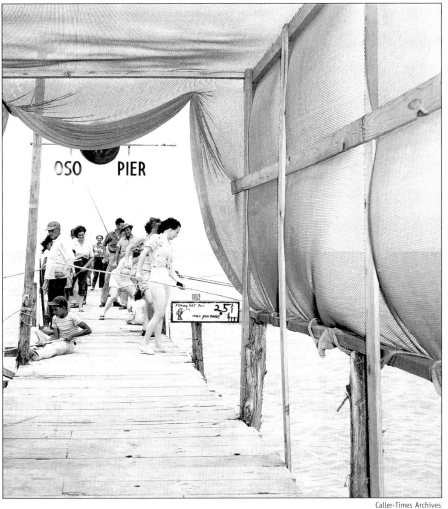

Caller-Times Archives

Oso Pier, c. 1950
The Oso Pier at the south end of Ocean Drive was built in 1948 by Jack Maddux.

Caller-Times Archives

Causeway, 1950

Cars line up on June 17 for the opening of the new $1.7 million Padre Island Causeway (later renamed the JFK Causeway). A total of 4,800 cars passed the Flour Bluff toll gate in the first 36 hours. This shot was taken from the toll gate, looking west toward Corpus Christi.

U.S. Corps of Engineers/Caller-Times Archives

A dredge working south from Corpus Christi and another working north from Brownsville chew on the last segment of the Intracoastal Waterway in 1949. The completed channel was opened to commerce on June 18, 1949.

Caller-Times Archives

Caller-Times Archives

1950

John B. Harney, sheriff of Nueces County from 1939 to 1953, holds the school bell for the old Nuecestown School. He said he hated the bell so much that on his last day of school he stole it from the teacher, a Miss Blanchard.

Lower North Broadway, c. 1950

The most famous newsman in Corpus Christi history — after Eli Merriman, founder of the *Caller* — was Bob McCracken, who wrote the Crow's Nest column that appeared on Page One for more than 20 years. As the author of the column, he was known as The Lookout. He became managing editor of the *Caller* in 1941 and then of both papers in 1945. He died on Oct. 29, 1958, at the age of 47. Some urged that the city's new high bridge be named the Lookout Bridge as a memorial to the late Bob McCracken.

Padre Island, 1950

The beach is packed with visitors on July 4, the first holiday after the opening of the new Padre Island Causeway two weeks before. The island, which had been relatively inaccessible for much of its history, suddenly became Corpus Christi's newest playground.

Peoples Street at Water, 1952

When it opened in 1913, the Nueces Hotel was the largest building south of San Antonio. The hotel became a center of civic and social activity for South Texas. The St. Cecilia Orchestra played nightly for dancing during the summer months. The hotel was enlarged with a 103-room wing in 1928. It was owned by South Texas rancher W.W. Jones. The grand old hotel became a retirement home before it was torn down in 1971.

Caller-Times Archives

Ada Wilson was a dominant figure in Corpus Christi's social and cultural life in the 1940s and '50s. She was best known as the founder of the Ada Wilson Hospital for Crippled Children, which began operations in 1938. Her husband Sam. E. Wilson (photo at right) moved to Corpus Christi in 1936 and, he said in one interview, he hit 44 producing wells in a row before drilling a dry hole. One of his earliest wells was in his own backyard on Shell Road.

Carl Graf/Caller-Times Archives

Agnes Street, c. 1950

Dancers at the Galvan Ballroom. Probably the Ralph Galvan Orchestra playing for a Sunday night dance.

Doc McGregor Photo/Galvan Collection
Texas A&M University-Corpus Christi

Caller-Times Archives

1954

George B. Parr, the 'Duke of Duval,' attracted the attentions of *Caller-Times* reporters in the 1950s, who began looking into widespread corruption in Duval County. Parr and cronies were found guilty of mail fraud in 1957, but their convictions were overturned by the Supreme Court. After Parr was convicted again in 1975, he committed suicide rather than go to jail.

Caller-Times Archives

Lower North Broadway, c. 1955

Caller-Times reporters C.W. Carpenter and Bill Walraven (standing, left to right) discuss a story with the city editor, John Anderson.

Napoleon's Hat

A new era opened for Corpus Christi when the Harbor Bridge was built to replace the bascule bridge that spanned the entrance to the port.

When the port opened in 1926, the bascule was an engineering marvel, the city's pride and joy and the centerpiece of the new port. But the 97-foot-wide opening was too narrow for the ever-larger ships arriving at the port. It had to be shut down numerous times when ships collided with the sides of the bridge. It was also a major annoyance for motorists stopped while the bascule was raised.

Efforts to solve the bottleneck began in the 1930s and intensified in the 1950s. The question that dominated the city was whether to build a tunnel or a bridge. The answer was decided by the State Highway Commission, which said it would pay the costs of building a bridge, provided the city paid for the right-of-way, but it would not pay for a tunnel. That decided the issue.

Bridge construction began in June, 1956 and was completed in 1959. The Harbor Bridge was opened to traffic on Oct. 23, 1959. It soon gained a nickname from sailors, who said its distinctive shape looked like Napoleon's Hat. It became the dominant feature of the city's skyline.

Bayfront, 1954

A U.S. Navy vessel approaches the port entrance at the bascule bridge.

Caller-Times Archives

Bayfront, 1959

Concrete finishers work on the roadway in February, 1959, as the high bridge nears completion. Four workers were killed during the construction of the bridge.

Caller-Times Archives

Bayfront, 1957

Work proceeds on the high bridge after construction was halted due to a shortage of material. Construction work began in May, 1956. More than 20 miles of pilings were pounded into the ground for the piers that supported gigantic pre-stressed concrete girders. The pilings were driven from September 1956 until February 1958.

Caller-Times Archives

Bayfront, 1959
Construction of the Harbor Bridge was started on each side of the ship channel with the cantilever trusses meeting in the middle. When the two spans met, they were off by a few inches, which had been expected. One side was jacked up until the two spans fell into line.

Photo by John Maxwell/Caller-Times Archives

Bayfront, 1959

Traffic waits while the bascule bridge opens to allow a vessel to leave the port turning basin on the day before the new Harbor Bridge was dedicated. The bascule was the pride of the city when it began operations in 1926, but it soon became a bottleneck for ships entering and leaving the port and for auto traffic entering and leaving the city.

Bayfront, 1959

The first car leads the way across the Harbor Bridge after it was dedicated on Oct. 23, 1959. More than 42,000 vehicles crossed over the new bridge in its first 24 hours. The name Harbor Bridge was chosen from hundreds of suggestions. Two other names considered were Corpus Christi Bridge and Lookout Bridge.

Caller-Times Archives

Caller-Times Archives

1959

Doc McGregor looks at a blowup of one of his most famous photographs — the frigate Constitution as tugs eased it through the bascule bridge opening to the port turning basin in 1932. McGregor positioned himself atop a signal tower near the port entrance while an assistant rode the bascule bridge up. But the assistant's pictures were lost when, in his excitement, he dropped the film in hypo instead of developer, ruining the roll.

Bayfront, 1959

Doc McGregor stands in front of the bascule bridge on the eve of the dedication of Corpus Christi's new Harbor Bridge. McGregor had a permanent pass allowing him to "ride" the bridge to get aerial photos of ships entering and leaving the port. McGregor, a chiropractor, also owned photo studios, did free lance photography for the *Caller-Times*, and for years was the official port photographer.

Then & NOW

Peoples and Schatzel, 1907

Looking from the bluff to the bay, Market Hall stands between Peoples and Schatzel streets. Market Hall was built in 1871 at a cost of $10,000. The lower floor on the west end was divided into stalls used by butchers and vendors. The second floor housed city offices and an auditorium/dance hall. The city's volunteer firemen operated out of the building.

Caller-Times Archives

. . . 1935

On the site of the old Market Hall is the city's three-story City Hall, built in 1911. In the middle foreground, across Mesquite Street from City Hall, is the State National Bank with a round dome over its front entrance.

Doc McGregor/Caller-Times Archives

Then & **NOW**

... 1954

In the 19 years since the 1935 photo, the view has changed dramatically. At the bottom of Peoples Street, one of the two T-heads has replaced the Pleasure Pier. The dominant buildings at the top of the photo are still the Nueces Hotel and the Jones Building. The 1911 city hall, is undergoing renovation to become La Retama Library.

... 2002

A "vest-pocket" park at the bottom of the photo, between Peoples and Schatzel, shows where Market Hall and the 1911 City Hall once stood. Across from the park on Peoples (left) is the Lovenskiold Building, a vacant derelict. The Furman Building on Peoples now has a front of shade trees. Down Peoples Street the Jones Building still stands. Hotels and high-rise bank buildings block the view of the T-head and the bay.

Then
&NOW

**Chaparral Street,
1946**

A large turnout honored
Admiral Chester W.
Nimitz of Texas, fleet
admiral and theater
commander in the Pacific,
on June 18. In his speech,
Nimitz said Corpus
Christi would always be
"a Navy town."

Carl Graf/Caller-Times Archives

. . . 2002

From the same viewpoint
today (a multi-level
parking garage where the
Nueces Hotel once stood),
the 400 block of
Chaparral presents a more
tranquil scene. The
Nimitz parade made it
look busier than usual,
but still, this was the
commercial center of the
city in the 1940s. The
Medical Professional
Building (left), Center
Theatre, and the
Lichtenstein/Frost
building are still there.
One notable difference
between the 1946 and
2002 photos is that the
city in the early 1980s
planted trees at downtown
intersections to make the
streets more
people-friendly.

Paul Iverson/Caller-Times

Then&NOW

Caller-Times Archives

Bayfront, 1941

The new Shoreline Boulevard was opened to traffic on March 29. Memorial Coliseum would later be built on the left foreground.

Paul Iverson/Caller-Times

Shoreline Boulevard, 2002

With the Coliseum dominating the median and the boulevard divided between northbound and southbound lanes, Shoreline today presents quite a contrast to the 1941 photo.

Then&**NOW**

Caller-Times Archives

Leopard at Broadway, 1918

Residences once lined the bluff along Upper Broadway. The bluff improvement project was completed in 1913. The home at the intersection of Leopard and Broadway was the Redmond house; it later was moved next to Spohn Hospital to use as a nurses' dorm. The other homes, starting across Leopard on the left, were occupied by the McCampbell, Barnes, Thomas, Weil and Spohn families. Farther down were the Richard King, John Kenedy, and Mifflin Kenedy homes. To the right of the Redmond house was the First Presbyterian Church. On the right side, at Lower Broadway and Starr, is the federal courthouse.

Paul Iverson/Caller-Times

Leopard at Broadway, 2002

Towering office and bank buildings today occupy Upper Broadway where the city's mansions once stood.

Then&NOW

Caller-Times Archives

Bayfront, 1907

Panoramic shot, taken from the top of the Pavilion Hotel, on a pier off Taylor Street. The square building on the water (upper left) was the Ladies Pavilion. The building on a pier on the right side was the Natatorium. The Seaside Hotel, with its arbor of salt cedars, is to the right of the Pavilion Hotel pier. The piers and houses on the waterfront were damaged or destroyed in the 1916 and 1919 hurricanes.

Paul Iverson/Caller-Times

Bayfront, 2002

Today's bayfront is dramatically different with the addition of the marina, seawall and high-rise buildings along Shoreline. The bayfront improvement project, completed in 1941, extended the city into the bay from Water Street.

Index

Partners in Progress

H-E-B

H-E-B opened the first store in Corpus Christi in 1931 on Mesquite Street. H-E-B's commitment to freshest products, great people and outstanding customer service have remained top priorities through the years, although styles, locations and products have changed.

H-E-B opened at 3133 S. Alameda in September 1949. This store was the first to incorporate the "supermarket" design with wide aisles, increased product variety and the first general merchandise department.

Partners in Progress

H-E-B stores have continually evolved to ensure we offer a great shopping experience. Since 1931, there have been approximately 40 different H-E-B stores in Corpus Christi.

Community involvement has been important since H-E-B first began in 1905. Returning 5% of its pretax income to nonprofit organizations, the company is committed to supporting the communities we serve.

THE OFFICERS AND PERSONNEL
OF THE
H. E. BUTT GROCERY COMPANY
CORDIALLY INVITE YOU TO ATTEND
THE OPENING OF THEIR NEWEST
H. E. B. FOOD STORE
KOSTORYZ AND GOLLIHAR ROADS
CORPUS CHRISTI, TEXAS

OPEN FOR BUSINESS
MONDAY, 8:00 A. M.
JULY 19TH, 1954

Old Corpus Christi

About the editor

Murphy D. Givens is a native Texan, born in Gatesville, who grew up and attended public schools and college in Alabama. He worked as reporter and editor at newspapers in Alabama, Michigan, and Mississippi before joining the *Caller-Times* in 1981. He is the Viewpoints Editor, sits on the Editorial Board, and has written more than 200 columns on Corpus Christi and South Texas history. His radio commentary on local history airs each Friday on KEDT-FM. He is married and has two children.

Project staff

Murphy D. Givens, project editor
Fernando Ortiz Jr., page designer
James Simmons, cover designer
Frank Lemos, photo scanner

Additional thanks to the following people who helped in the project:
Steve Arnold, Libby Averyt, Charles L. Baskin, Herb Canales, Grace Charles, Miranda Dvorak,
Cecil Ferrell, Deborah W. Fisher, Laura Z. Garcia, Norma Gonzalez, Patricia Herrera, Paul Iverson,
Kevin Kerrigan, Tom Kreneck, Geraldine McGloin, Mary Lou Morris, Patricia Murphy,
Margaret Neu, Barbara Oliver, Harold Ong, Brooks Peterson, Larry L. Rose,
Steve Stewart, George Tuley, Jan Weaver, William F. White.